DATE DUE

A FINE WILL BE CHARGED FOR EACH
OVERDUE MATERIAL.

GENCO

ARCIMBOLDO THE MARVELOUS

ARCIMBOLDO
THE MARVELOUS

by

André Pieyre de Mandiargues

Conception by Yasha David

Harry N. Abrams, Inc., Publishers, New York

Library of Congress Catalogue Card Number: 77-25439
Copyright © 1977 by Editions Robert Laffont, Paris

Published in 1978 by Harry N. Abrams, Incorporated, New York.

Printed and bound in Switzerland

The list of paintings by Arcimboldo could not have been compiled without assistance from the following, whose cooperation is gratefully acknowledged: Ulf Abel, Sven G. Alfons, Jean-Pierre Cuzin, Jean-Marc Gutton, Ebba Hanson, Eva Hökerberg, Jan Ivarsson, Thord Plaenge Jacobson, Ulf G. Johnsson, Jitka Klingenberg, Dr. Georg J. Kugler, Robert Lebel, Dr. Ake Meyerson, Professor Alfredo Puerari, and Nicole Vasseur.

Arcimboldo's known drawings, which are not reproduced in this book, are: *Self-Portrait* (Narodni Galerie, Prague), *Italian Peasant Woman* (Prado, Madrid), *Profile of Rudolf II, King of Bohemia* (Narodni Muzeum, Prague), *Profile of Rudolf II, Holy Roman Emperor* (Narodni Muzeum, Prague), 145 Sketches for Headdresses, Costumes, Chariots, and Sleighs (Uffizi Gallery, Florence), and 14 sketches for the fresco series *Silkworm Breeding* (Museum of Fine Arts, Boston).

Yasha David

CONTENTS

LIST OF ILLUSTRATIONS

Self-Portrait

He was a marvel, without a doubt. But my first question concerning this sixteenth-century Milanese painter—in whose work I have long had the keenest interest—is, what is his real name? How shall I, or should I, refer to him in the following pages? A touch of the cabala is inseparable from the Imperial courts of Maximilian II and Rudolf II at Vienna and Prague, where our artist was court painter, yet it is curious that his name is spelled differently even today in the two books recently written about him. The first—written in Italian by Benno Geiger, probably while he was in Venice—is entitled *I dipinti ghiribizzosi di Giuseppe Arcimboldi* (Florence, 1954); the second, in French, by F. Legrand and A. Sluys, bears the title *Giuseppe Arcimboldo et les arcimboldesques* (Brussels, 1955). Elsewhere, as in the excellent *Die Welt als Labyrinth* by G. R. Hocke (Hamburg, 1957), the two spellings are used concurrently, or indifferently. And although in the painter's native Italy his name is most often written Arcimboldi (as I have myself), the usage in most other countries is to prefer the form Arcimboldo.

In several official documents the painter signed himself or was designated with the Latin form Josephus Arcimboldus, which makes me think that the declension of his Latinized name may have led to the subsequent confusion in its final syllable. After all, the artist's own *Self-Portrait,* the blue drawing in the Narodni Galerie of Prague, bears the inscription "Joseffi Arcimboldi." Yet the painter's epitaph (lost long since with the destruction of the church of San Pietro della Vigna in Milan), was it not addressed to "Joseph Arcimboldo Viro Integerrimo Pictori Clarissimo" by his "most intimate" friend Cesari Besozzi? And in the public health register of Milan we find the death certificate of one Joseph Arcimboldi, deceased July 11, 1593, "at age 66 or thereabouts, of suppression of urine and kidney stones, with no sign of plague"—a document which, incidentally, provides us with the year of the artist's birth, about 1527, more precisely than is often the case for his contemporaries.

The Jesuit author Paolo Morigia, another close friend of the artist, occasionally refers to the *casa Arcimbolda,* or "House of Arcimbolda," in his treatise *Della nobilità di Milano* (Milan, 1595). The name has probably a Germanic origin, like all Italian names with endings derived from *bald* or *bold* (usually interpreted to mean "daring" or "courageous"). Another book by Morigia, *Historia dell'Antichità di Milano* (Venice, 1592), informs us that the painter traced his family back to a mythical ancestor, a certain Saxon knight called Saitfrid (Siegfried) who served the emperor Charlemagne, and who supposedly discovered a silver mine in a forest—whence the etymology of "Arcimboldo" from *Erz im Wald* ("Ore in the forest"). In his *Milano nobilissima; Famiglie celebre d'Italia* (Milan, 1819) Pompeo Litta, a nineteenth-century genealogist, scrutinizes the Arcimboldo family tree and finds that the painter's branch had a poor reputation: Giuseppe's father, Biagio—whose portrait in profile, a lovely charcoal drawing by Bernardino Luini, is in the British Museum—was a lesser craftsman in the workshop of Milan Cathedral; his grandfather was not a legitimate child. The celebrated "nobility" that Giuseppe seemed to value so much was acquired by

The Librarian

the work of his own hands, like that of all the true (meaning the first) aristocrats: in 1592 Rudolf II, Arcimboldo's Imperial patron, made him a count palatine, the same title that Emperor Charles IV had conferred upon Petrarch in Prague more than two centuries before. In the early days of the Bohemian capital, aristocracies of the pen and brush were not differentiated from those of the sword.

The fame of this painter, oddly enough, lasted only about a century, but variations on his name continued to multiply. The records of the cathedral workshop in Milan refer to his decorative work under the names Giuseppe Arcimboldi, Joseph Arcimboldo, and Joseph de Arcimboldis. Arnaboldo, as the name appears on the payroll of Como Cathedral for a tapestry sketch, is surely a scribe's error, but similar records reveal more variants: Joseph Arczimbaldo (Prague, 1565); and several instances of Joseph Arzimboldo in Vienna during that and the following year. Subsequently "Joseph Arcimboldo" (or "-baldo") appears most often, but this does not prevent the occurrence of Arcimboldoff and Arczimbalda (in Prague).

References to Joseph Arcimboldo crop up on the passport for his return trip to Italy in 1566, on the certificate by which Maximilian II legitimized Giuseppe's bastard son Benedetto, on Rudolf II's confirmation of his nobility, and on his appointment as count palatine—although "Arcimboldi" reappears on the artist's death certificate in Milan. We should remember that one important document, the 1621 inventory of the Imperial collections in Prague, lists his works under "Arcimboldo." In short, prevailing custom and sheer frequency have determined my choice to speak here of a marvelous artist named Arcimboldo. It was more likely his justifiable pride, I think, than his modesty that made him so apparently unconcerned about the all-too-numerous spellings of his name.

We know little about his youth and apprenticeship, a matter which does not seem crucial to me. At twenty-two he received his first fee as an artist, working with his father, Biagio, on the decoration of Milan Cathedral. This never-completed enterprise was—and, unless I am mistaken, still is—an inexhaustible source of manna for Lombard artists. In 1551 Arcimboldo painted the five coats of arms that were presented to the cathedral by the king of Bohemia (Ferdinand I; in 1556 he was elected emperor), a fact perhaps notable because the monarch may have become interested in the young artist through this commission. I see no great significance in his sketches for stained-glass windows in Milan Cathedral (executed by the German glassmaker known as Corrado de Mochis), or in his drawings for tapestries in Como Cathedral, except that the latter were woven by the Flemish Jan and Luigi Carcher in their tapestry workshop in Ferrara, which probably prompted Arcimboldo to make trips to the city of the dukes of Este. The atmosphere in Ferrara was known to be extravagant and fantastic, in contrast with the spiritual climate prevailing in Milan after the defeat of Ludovico il Moro in 1499, the subsequent French occupation, and the outbreak of plague early in the sixteenth century.

What seems worthier of close examination is the example provided by Leonardo da Vinci for

Spring

Giuseppe Arcimboldo and all young Lombard artists, his philosophical as well as his pictorial work. Leonardo had spent some twenty-four years in Milan, all told, before he moved to France in 1516, to die in Amboise in 1519. Thanks to personal as well as professional contacts between Arcimboldo's father and the Luini family of artists, Giuseppe must have seen Leonardo's work earlier than most artists did. Aurelio Luini kept like relics the sketches in the notebook Leonardo had left to Bernardino Luini, Aurelio's father, and certainly showed Arcimboldo those admirable monsters, those caricatured features embodying time itself, those hybrids of flora and fauna meshing bizarrely into the human face. These drawings fascinated Arcimboldo and remained in his memory all his life. Adolfo Venturi, in his monumental *Storia dell'arte italiana* (vol. IX, Milan, 1934), correctly notes of Arcimboldo that "of the great Leonardo's students, none could match this later disciple's ability to grasp and render the motion of the molecules, the internal structure of animal form. Indeed, the hand of Leonardo seems to have guided

that of Arcimboldo." At the risk of banality, we must reiterate that Leonardo's philosophy was a naturalistic one, which alone lies behind the meaning of his comical sketches, his "jokes." And we must consider Arcimboldo's works from the same point of view; he sought and found his own achievements by using that framework to interpret his message. *Hostinato rigore*, "determined severity," was Leonardo's motto, we must remember, and Arcimboldo could well have taken it for himself once he was past his experimental period, had his self-pride not been tinged with a secret respect. The phrase is apt insofar as we see Arcimboldo revealed in his works. These are few for a lifetime that was by no means short; it is worth noting, because his limited output underscores the similarity to Leonardo's. In Leonardo's manuscript sketches at the Institut de France, and in the pages of his codices, one sees his attempt to represent all the possible structures produced by nature, as well as all the contrivances that the human mind could imagine: "The true form that explains them," wrote Leonardo, not wishing to distinguish too much

Summer

among them, and spurred by what Paul Valéry termed "the delights of construction." This also sums up Arcimboldo, as I see him.

But his wholly original success came after detaching himself from the Luini family and striking out on his own. Granted, Leonardo's genius was a revelation to him, but his career officially began with what one might call a stroke of luck: the invitation extended in 1562 by Emperor Ferdinand I, king of Bohemia and younger brother of Charles V, to come to Vienna and serve as court portraitist and copyist. From that year until 1587—a period spanning the reigns of the emperors Ferdinand I, Maximilian II, and Rudolf II—the artist lived at the courts of Vienna and especially Prague except for a few professional excursions to Bavaria and Italy. After he returned to Italy he died in his native Milan in 1593, as we mentioned above. Arcimboldo's face sticks in one's mind more accurately than does his real name; he left two self-portraits which we must still respond to four centuries later—the distinguished and beautifully structured face, the expression bespeaking

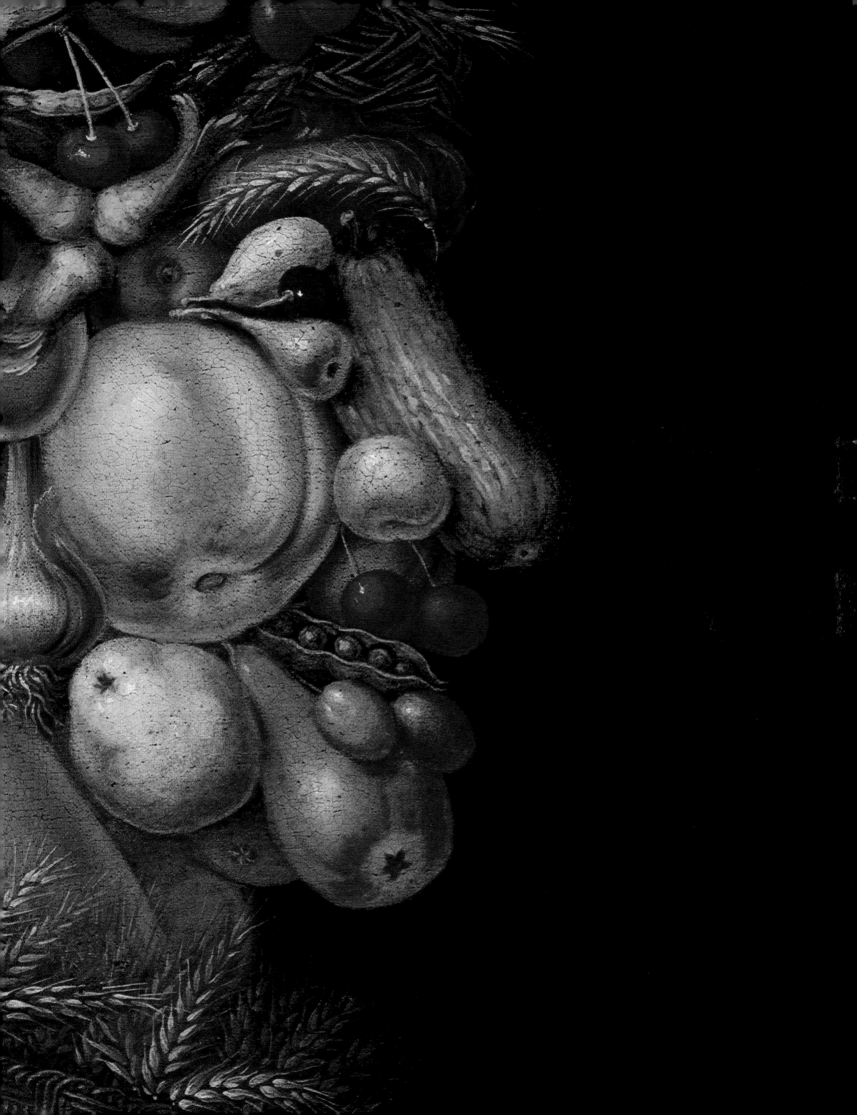

intelligence, nobility, and a somewhat melancholy seriousness. A philosopher's face, one is tempted to say; certainly not the face of a joker, as the swarm of fools whom I am here pleased to refute have summarily judged this great painter to be. It is the face of a Renaissance artist whose hand, for all its deftness, is controlled by the mind, and of an intellectual artist, as borne out by the singular nature of his work. One of the self-portraits is a painting (page 9), its whereabouts unknown today; the other is a drawing on blue-toned paper in the Narodni Galerie in Prague. The belief that the Prague drawing was preparatory to the painting strikes me as incorrect: the drawing is in full-face, whereas the subject in the painting is in three-quarter view, and looks in a different direction; his beard seems longer, too, in the painting, and his age less advanced. Both portraits reveal a curious asymmetry in Arcimboldo's face, the right side having higher color than the left. Benno Geiger dates the painting in 1570, but I find unconvincing his reason for this statement. In any event the painting (whose more youthful aspect

Autumn

points to its being the earlier) as well as the drawing were both probably completed during first the royal, then the Imperial reign of Maximilian II, from 1562 to 1576. They have additional importance because they are the only realistic portraits made indisputably by Arcimboldo that remain to us.

Nothing has survived of his work as portraitist-copyist under Ferdinand I, or as official portraitist under Maximilian II and Rudolf II, that can be attributed to him with certainty, or even probability. Presumably he began his appointment by tediously copying court portraits, however boring and mediocre they were in quality, and it is doubtful that he tried to improve them. There is mention of a large family portrait in which, at Maximilian's behest, he assembled the likenesses of all the Hapsburgs, living or dead; we must confess to no great sorrow that this illustrious group portrait has disappeared—although the intriguing look of degeneracy shown by most members of that noble family would surely have suited Arcimboldo's taste for the monstrous, had he been given free rein.

Yet his two self-portraits enchant us by their
poetic realism, in the manner of many faces
by Leonardo.

Actually, aside from a few royal or Imperial
portraits in what was then the traditional court style
of portraiture, and thus indistinguishable today, we
have reason to believe that Arcimboldo's major
work, particularly in Prague, lay in arranging and
enriching the famous *Wunderkammern*, the
collections of art and curiosities of Maximilian II
and Rudolf II. The factor of curiosity—whose
extreme limits verge on pathological
psychology—has always seemed to me one of
man's essential virtues, worthy of being added to
the three theological and four cardinal virtues. But
rarely have monarchs displayed curiosity to the
degree that Maximilian and Rudolf did, and artists
such as Leonardo and Arcimboldo. So much has
been written about the Imperial collections in this
period, how they were filled beyond the imaginable
with marvels natural and artificial, that I shall not
add anything here except to say that "cultural" and

Winter

"raw" art, so to speak, were brought together on equal footing: magic objects from the world over cordially rubbed shoulders with Christian relics and Roman Catholic paraphernalia selected for their unusual or precious appearance. I think I was seeing an accumulation of treasures comparable to those in the *Wunderkammern* (except for the Catholic objects, which were excluded) whenever I visited André Breton, and each time I rejoiced at the fantastic display built around him, the paintings, sculpture, and objects of every sort and origin that made up his astonishing collection.

In these *Wunderkammern* Arcimboldo undoubtedly spent, not to say wasted, much time while he was a pensioned artist of the Prague emperors, but it was exactly there and then that his art found its characteristic and original creation, the "composite head," which blossomed with the brilliance that we all know. On this subject the matter of its sources is intensely debated. There are, to be sure, many Indian miniatures showing animals, usually elephants, horses, and antelopes, that overlap with other animals or with human

figures, including lovers. Of those painted before Arcimboldo's time, some might have caught the painter's eye in the Vienna or Prague collections. And in Italy he could have seen a fanciful monster of that sort in the miniatures of a fifteenth-century Armenian manuscript in the library on the Isola di San Lazzaro degli Armeni, near Venice. Further back in time, the ancient Romans, if not the Greeks as well, used the same procedure for engraving certain types of cameos, decorating vases, and composing mosaics; I have seen examples of these in the Archeological Museum at Naples. Roger Caillois points to decorated initials in fifteenth-century manuscripts and incunabula; the illuminators made whimsical composites of men, animals, and plants that retain the form of letters, their curious contortions notwithstanding, and he suggests that Arcimboldo may have borrowed these strategems, by which, he says, "the eye is invited to decompose and to reconstruct the total image." And we should remember that children and primitive and unsophisticated peoples have always played at making mosaics or masks on a simpler plane that

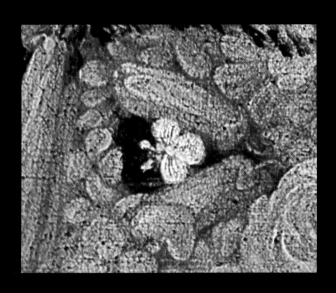

Spring (detail of eye)

bring together fruit, flowers, pebbles, or shells more or less artfully; usually these creations are fragile, but certain durable examples might have had a place in the Imperial collections. Finally I return to Leonardo; his drawings often show hybrids from every natural realm, and his writings advise whoever wishes to concoct an imaginary or monstrous being to assemble parts of the bodies of all the creatures he knows.

All well and good, but the crux of the issue or problem lies elsewhere. The evidence shows that a number of "arcimboldesques" existed before Arcimboldo's authentic works, and he may have been inspired by seeing certain of them. Others, moreover, were made subsequently, especially in the fifty years following his death; most of them were the offspring of his work, in ever-worsening quality—and such imitations will always be with us. But between these two broad currents of "arcimboldesques" there occurs the marvelous, dazzling zenith that is the oeuvre of Arcimboldo himself.

It is this work and this artist alone that interests

me, and so intensely that I wish to steer the spectator away from the "arcimboldesques." Here I refer to them only to combat feeble attributions that have been made in hopes of belittling or ignoring the masterly art of the painter. At the same time I will try to reinstate certain exclusions; such treatment in at least one case, the magnificent *Flora* in Paris, is fundamentally negated by the emotion that her beauty raises in us when we see the work. In painting as in poetry, whether the artist is Arcimboldo or a Baudelaire or Rimbaud, judgments of originality must be based primarily on a certain sense of the beautiful. It is only when I make myself look with the vision that is André Breton's that I sometimes dare pronounce an opinion—a lesson I take the liberty of recommending to many in the cultural professions.

To Arcimboldo's work for the Imperial collections of art and curiosities should be added another post that the rulers of the Empire entrusted to him: "Master of Court Festivals and Masquerades," a title that in German conveys a degree of solemnity,

Festivals provided the greatest diversion from political difficulties in Vienna and especially Prague during the second half of the sixteenth century, when the disquieting horoscopes cast at the birth of the Imperial princes were mercilessly confirmed as their reigns unfolded. The court lapdogs—those artists, lords and ladies, scholars, and high officials who hung about the king of Bohemia or the so-called Holy Roman Emperor—packed together for a perpetual succession of parades, pageants, tournaments, exotic riding spectacles (devised by Arcimboldo), and indoor or outdoor entertainments. Taking place in the palaces, gardens, streets, and squares of Vienna, a city whose architecture suggested a theater set, they made it into a carnival of the four seasons, the spring, summer, autumn, and winter that became the principal subjects for Arcimboldo's inspiration. Similar festivities that spread to the Bohemian capital helped to make the people bear their woes more patiently, and it is not impossible that the emperors Maximilian and Rudolf made conscious use of such occasions to distract the

population from the current religious struggles between Catholicism and the Reformation. And in Prague the terrible repression of the Hussite heresy that began with the fifteenth-century antipope, John XXIII, was too recent to be forgotten.

But I return to Arcimboldo by way of his designs for these festivities, drawings of headdresses, costumes, groups of people, fabulous monsters, triumphal chariots, and sleighs. A red morocco portfolio in the Uffizi Gallery in Florence contains an astonishing collection of 145 drawings, presented by the artist to Rudolf II in 1585 before he returned finally to Italy. And his fourteen drawings in pen and wash in the Museum of Fine Arts, Boston, though more strictly constructed, are hardly different in style; they are scenes of silkworm culture that make it look like a charming game. The gracefulness and Leonardesque suavity of touch in all these drawings suffice to relegate to its rightful place the "kitchen" drawing of *The Cook* in the Ecole des Beaux-Arts in Paris; its artist can safely return to his earlier classification as "anonymous Flemish or German artist." But close

at hand to the beautiful *Self-Portrait* drawing in Prague's Narodni Galerie, there are in the Narodni Muzeum in Prague two drawings, both very moving, which depict Rudolf II on his coronation day in Regensburg, in 1576. Arcimboldo's beloved emperor appears relatively at ease beneath his light crown as King of Bohemia, but he is like a poor moonstruck clown in the other, crushed by his crown as Holy Roman Emperor.

We can add that for the various hydraulic mechanisms which Arcimboldo invented and built as "Master of Festivals" he only followed the example of Leonardo. Much more original and enigmatic are his two inventions in the realm of music, the "perspective lute" and the "harpsichord of colors." We know that the first of these existed, since such an instrument appears in the 1621 inventory of the collections in Hradcany Castle. About the second we can read at length in *Il Figino,* the "Mantuan dialogue" written by the canon Gregorio Comanini, one of Arcimboldo's closest friends and his most intelligent commentator after his return to Italy. The discussion is among Stefano

Guazzo, Ascanio Martinengo, and the painter Ambrogio Figino himself; we are told that the young viol player Mauro Cremonese, instructed by Arcimboldo, found on the "color harpsichord" all the consonances noted in colors by the artist on a sheet of paper. Rudolf II undoubtedly observed this experiment and the sessions that followed. In an essay added to Benno Geiger's book, the musicologist Lionello Levi asserts that Arcimboldo's aim was to link up the optical and acoustical numbers according to the Pythagorean theories that were enjoying renewed favor among acoustical theoreticians and all who pursued the new musical humanism.

Even if this invention concerned only a notation or visual description of the auditory range, or a concrete realization of the correspondences between colors and sounds—from which, centuries later, Baudelaire too would draw inspiration—why should we not be greatly impressed by it? In the astounding diversity of all these activities, the many discoveries, games, and (as discussed later) the "philosophy," we could think that painting was

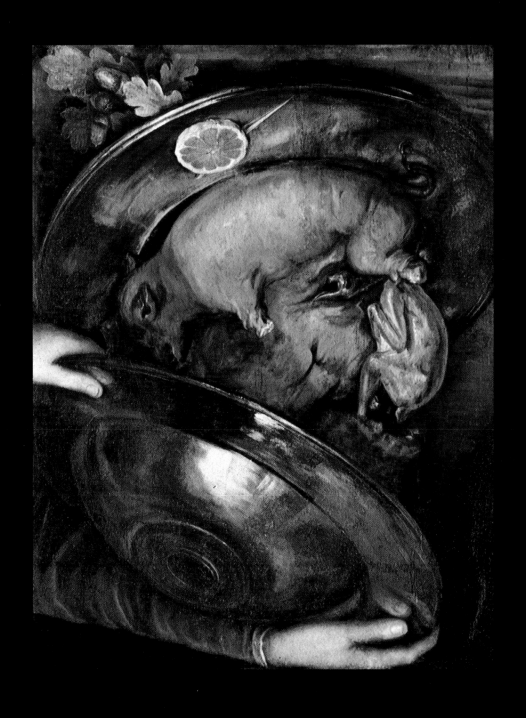

The Man in the Plate

almost ancillary in Arcimboldo's life—and much the same can be said of Leonardo, who left no greater number of completed works than Arcimboldo. Yet it is the painting of both artists that attests to the splendor of their existence, for Arcimboldo's works, too, are bearers of revelation.

Such a revelation I experienced myself in the autumn of 1931, while visiting the Kunsthistorisches Museum in Vienna. As I recall, I had come to look at the paintings by Bruegel; after a long time with them, I wandered by chance into the large rooms in which hung the sensual visions by the Mannerist school. Suddenly, as if touched by magic, I found myself before four paintings: *Winter* and *Summer* (from *The Four Seasons*), and *Fire* and *Water* (from *The Four Elements*). I could plainly see that their subjects were human heads composed of disparate objects that were natural in origin more often than man-made, but there was so much true genius in the arrangement of the components, such facility in the drawing, such brilliance and sensitivity in the colors, and such

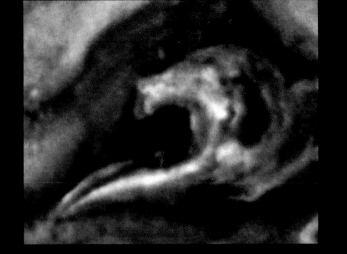

The Man in the Plate (detail of eye)

expressive power in the eyes that animated the immobile wriggling of these bizarre faces—it is not surprising that I was almost struck dumb on first discovering them. The author of these composite heads was a certain sixteenth-century Italian, Giuseppe Arcimboldo, unknown to me. When I wondered why I had not noticed these paintings before, on a Christmas visit in 1927 or 1928, I learned that they had been hung only recently, after having been a long time in storage. Let us hope that the authorities at the Louvre will soon follow the example of the Kunsthistorisches Museum's curators and bring into the light the four beautiful *Seasons* paintings by Arcimboldo that they own and that are reproduced here (pages 17 through 37). Their excuse, when asked, is that the works were acquired only a few years ago.

The greater part of Arcimboldo's oeuvre consists of two groups of four paintings each: *The Four Seasons (Spring, Summer, Autumn,* and *Winter)* and *The Four Elements (Air, Earth, Water,* and *Fire).* The original version of the first group, *The Four Seasons,* is dated 1563, during the reign

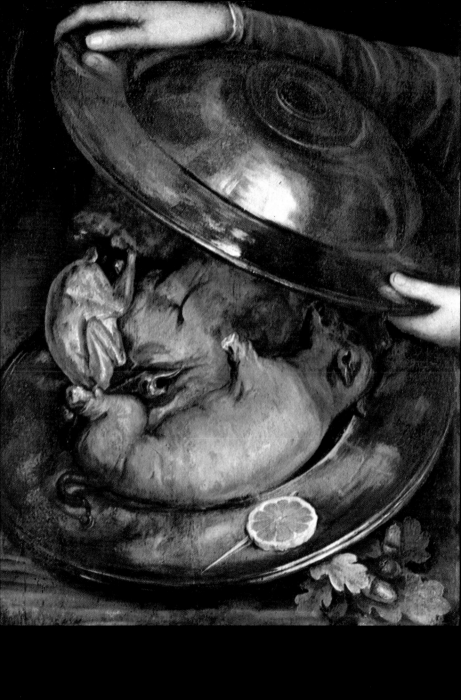

The Man in the Plate (inverted)

of Ferdinand I. Of its four paintings, the Kunst-historisches Museum owns two, the allegorical figures of *Summer* and *Winter; Spring,* recently rediscovered, is in Madrid's Real Academia de Bellas Artes de San Fernando, while *Autumn* remains missing. Are these Arcimboldo's earliest composite heads, or should that honor be reserved for the altogether astonishing *Librarian* (which I will discuss later)? The question is not yet resolved, it seems to me.

Without mentioning certain nearly contemporary copies, four versions of *The Four Seasons* appear to have indisputable authenticity. There is the incomplete series of 1563, described above, and another of 1572, from which *Spring* is missing. Two complete series are dated 1573. One of these sets was brought from Prague in 1620 by Queen Elizabeth of Bohemia, who was the daughter of James I of England, wife of the Elector Palatine Frederick V, and queen of Bohemia for the single winter of 1619–20; this series shortly entered the collection of the counts of Craven in England. The second, reproduced in this book (pages 17 through 37), was acquired by the Louvre in 1964; we note that Comanini alludes in *Il Figino* to a *scherzo* (possibly a sketch) by Arcimboldo of the four seasons united into one picture, which was apparently in Comanini's possession about 1590. Could the Louvre canvases have been cut from this painting before they were remounted? The question has been raised.

What seems certain is that the emperors Maximilian II and, especially, Rudolf II considered Arcimboldo's paintings to be "marvels," and sometimes gave one as a treasured gift to particular relatives or favorites, in which case the painter would be asked to undertake the re-creation of the absent "marvel." This accomplishment provided proof of the artist's genius and confirmed him in the dignity of his title, Imperial painter—rather like the court alchemists who justified their titles by occasionally conjuring up a small transmutation. It is probably a mistake to look upon Arcimboldo as an artist overwhelmed with commissions from either his "masters" or other clients. His powerful patrons charged him instead with such duties as organizing their ceremonies and festivals, or adding antiques to their collections—all of which, unfortunately, stood in the way of his painting.

But let us return to *The Four Seasons,* those "marvels" that the Louvre is so reluctant to display. Curiously, these four paintings are all framed within by painted garlands which are attached to the canvas: who put them on, or when, I cannot say. The argument that Arcimboldo had a taste for this sort of decoration, as seen in his youthful tapestry sketches, is not sufficient to hold him responsible here.

The anthropomorphic *Spring* (pages 17, 19), all leaves and flowers, is a still life that is very much alive. Two small dark fruits, apparently wild cherries, add sparkle to the eye, and two prickly wild strawberries rise below the lovely iris that serves as a corsage. Above the flowers of the headdress is a white lily in full bloom; another, still a drooping bud, makes the nose. The parted lips are little rosebuds voluptuously darkened. This wild burst of sensuality affords the first indication of

Air

the flawless drawing that avoids any hint of banality, the ingenuity of placing each object—all these bespeak the artist's obvious delight in his discoveries, a kind of rapture that he must have sensed just as we sense it in the completed works. Arcimboldo's art is literally ravishing: like a ravenous creature it carries us off.

Intensity of the same degree marks the three other heads in the *Seasons* series. *Summer* (pages 21, 23–25), the "king of seasons" as one used to say, is arranged with sovereign pleasure out of fruits (green grapes, plums, mulberries, a melon, hazelnuts, assorted pears, scarlet cherries, a wild black cherry for the eye, an opulent peach for the

Earth

cheek) and vegetables (ears of corn and wheat, bulbs of garlic, onions, peapods, eggplant, and various squashes, including a zucchini that makes a ponderous green nose fit for a Hapsburg). In place of *Spring*'s iris, a stalk of artichoke adorns *Summer*'s jacket of braided and woven wheat spikes. The date 1573 is seen on the shoulder, while the golden surface of the collar bears the artist's name proudly in raised letters: GIUSEPPE ARCIMBOLDO • F. Incidentally we point out here that the signature in the same place on a copy of *Summer,* probably contemporary (once in a Swedish collection), reads ARCIMBLDO—is the misspelling a scruple, or an unintentional admission of dishonesty? Finally we note the similarity of the splendid *Summer* to Arcimboldo's last or next-to-last masterpiece, *Portrait of Rudolf II as Vertumnus,* of about 1590 (pages 101 through 109).

The head of *Autumn* (pages 27, 29–31) rises from a split-up cask, bound with supple branches, that resembles a loose corset more than a bodice or cuirass; the ornament on its breast is a worm-eaten medlar with leaves. Made ruddy by the apple of the

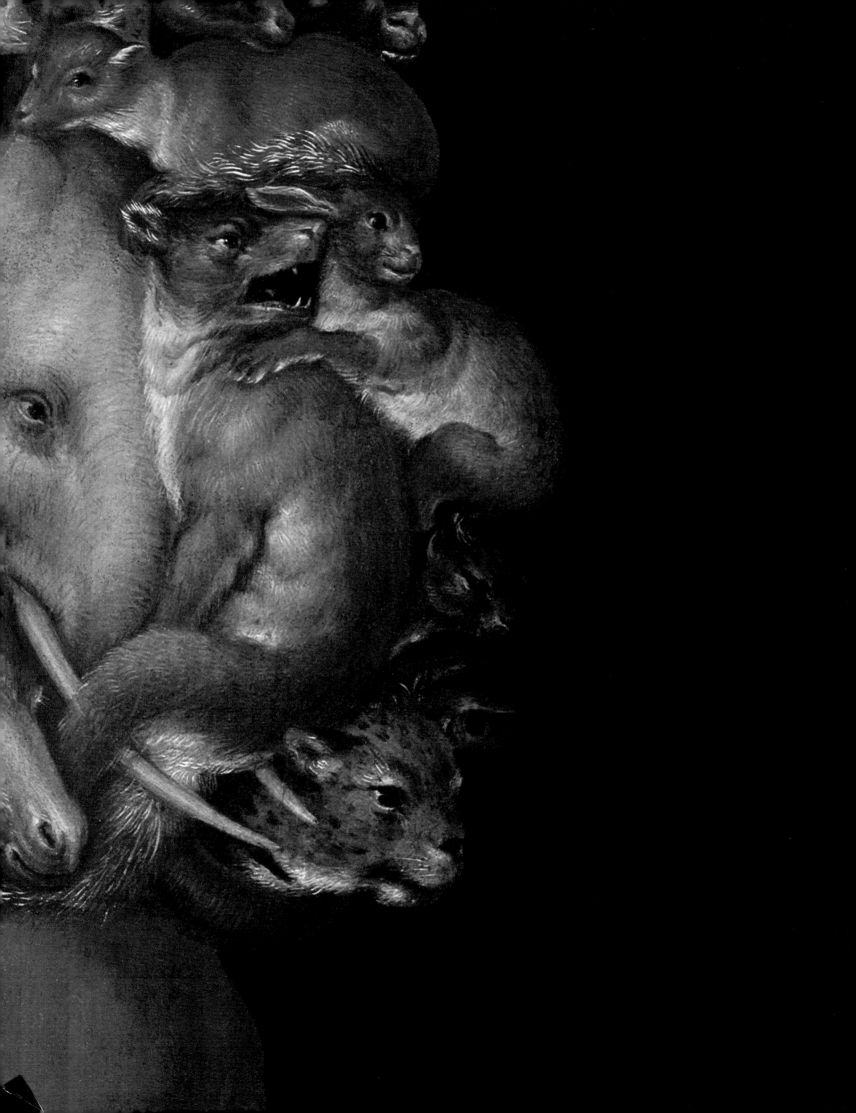

cheek, the pear of the nose, and the pomegranate chin, this is a Bacchic head: the hair, composed of bunches of ripe grapes and reddened vine leaves, is coiffed above with a huge pumpkin and nuts in their shells. A chestnut sticking out from its prickly burr is the tongue of this faunlike fellow; his gleaming eye is a blackberry coupled with a tiny toadstool; his ear is a red mushroom of the russula family; his earring, a split purple fig; his sideburns are wormwood. Various roots and tubers make the nape and throat, twin supports of this drunkenness or violence.

Winter is the least intricate of these composite heads and one of the artist's most successful marvels (pages 33, 35–37). The image is of an old and anthropomorphic chestnut stump, the bark cracked and overrun with ivy and afflicted with a tree fungus that looks like a mouth with twisted lips. But buried in a fissure in the dead wood is a sparkling eye which could only be the gleam of a gem, its fire icy and frightening. Matted wickerwork shelters the area where the shoulders should be and crosses a bit below the chest

ornament—this time a twig with a hanging lemon and orange, precious citrus fruits in the lifeless season.

The Four Seasons nearly sums up the work of Arcimboldo, his most celebrated accomplishment for us today as in the past. Thanks to numerous versions made by the artist himself and by copyists and imitators, this series is the most widely known. We might add here that they could be interpreted as four "demons" as well as four "masks," depending on whether the observer chooses to emphasize their philosophical (I could say metaphysical) or playful disposition.

In The Four Elements, inseparable from The Four Seasons and begun three years later, the composite-head technique is pushed to the extreme (pages 57 through 83). Each head utilizes a great many components, including in three cases the creatures that inhabit the element represented (birds in Air, four-legged mammals in Earth, and mostly fish, mollusks, and shellfish in Water). In Fire the painter uses flames, inflammable materials, lighting

devices, and objects related to incandescence and explosion.

Air (pages 57–59), as it is seen in a version that may be an original replica or an excellent contemporary copy, must surely be the least agreeable, the most aggressive, of all Arcimboldo's paintings. There is no inherent confusion, but this composite head can only be understood by a special effort of attention because the details imperiously dominate the overall design, details that are nothing but a multitude of birds' beaks and eyes. On the outspread peacock feathers that make up the upper torso the eyes seem to stare out at you by the hundred; the little heads in the headdress seem to be on the verge of tearing each other apart with their sharp beaks—before they turn on you as well. It is to Arcimboldo's honor that he perceived and rendered so well the cruel morphology of the bird kingdom four centuries earlier than our contemporary writers and film-makers.

Water (pages 68–69, 71), in Vienna's Kunsthistorisches Museum, is one of the artist's most magnificent compositions. It is evident that this allegory was not painted only for the assured purpose of bringing smiles to the emperor and his courtiers. All these sea creatures—from fish, crustacea, mollusks, reptiles, amphibians, and mammals down to starfish, shipworms, pearls, and coral—can be recognized and classified, in spite of their variations in size. Behind the sting-ray, the eye of this awesome face strikes me as being that of a moonfish with its mouth agape. The confidence we may have placed in Arcimboldo's critics will not be bolstered by the claim of two of these, that the creature whose legs form the eyelashes is a shrimp. Shrimp, indeed! This lovely crustacean is a squilla, or mantis prawn (*cannocchia* in Italian), which I well know, having often purchased them live in Venetian markets (a two- or three-minute boil is enough to bring out their flavor).

To the Kunsthistorisches Museum goes also the glory of possessing *Fire* (pages 77, 79–83, 85); like the two *Elements* just discussed, this portrait too looms menacingly from a dark background. *Fire*, the youngest of *The Four Elements*, owes nothing to flora or fauna. Crowned with burning

75

combustible fuses, matches of the time, a lighted oil lamp and burning candles, and below, of cannon, mortar, and pistol. The figure wears a beautiful necklace with the ram's-head pendant of the Order of the Golden Fleece—of which the figure's striking-steel nose and ear are themselves symbolic—leading one to believe that the live model (who surely existed) for this industrial still life was in actuality a Hapsburg prince. Engraved portraits suggest the violent Matthias as the most likely candidate—he dethroned his older brother Rudolf II in 1608 and held him captive during his last years—but Matthias was only nine years old when this flame-crowned Pluto was painted, which makes the hypothesis, alas, highly improbable. This is the only one of *The Four Elements* that is signed: we read on the cannon mouth, "Josephus Arcimboldus," and below, an abbreviation of "Milanensis" (this word, misread as "Utrensis," greatly intrigued the same critics who mistook a squilla for a shrimp).

The fourth element, *Earth* (pages 61, 63–65),

Fire

also known as *Grotesque Head* and *The Hunter,* hung for long in the Belvedere in Graz, Austria, from which it has now been sold. Although it differs somewhat in dimension from the two *Four Elements* panels in Vienna, its authenticity is not doubted. Comanini describes it at length in *Il Figino,* saying that it had been sent to the king of Spain—probably an error, unless he was speaking of a copy that went there and has since disappeared. The head of *Earth* is composed of mammals, more wild than domestic. A ram's fleece is spread so ostentatiously over the chest that one cannot help thinking once again of some high official in the Order of the Golden Fleece—the Imperial vice-chancellor (to quote Lomazzo), or the portrait of a Hapsburg: it could be Emperor Maximilian, given the heavy features that are anything but majestic. I find it interesting that the little monkey perched near the top of the skull and framed by the antlers of stag and elk has a curious resemblance to Arcimboldo himself as seen in his *Self-Portrait* (page 9)—not, as in the case of Hieronymus Bosch, a "monkey of God," but a "monkey of the Elements." And why not?

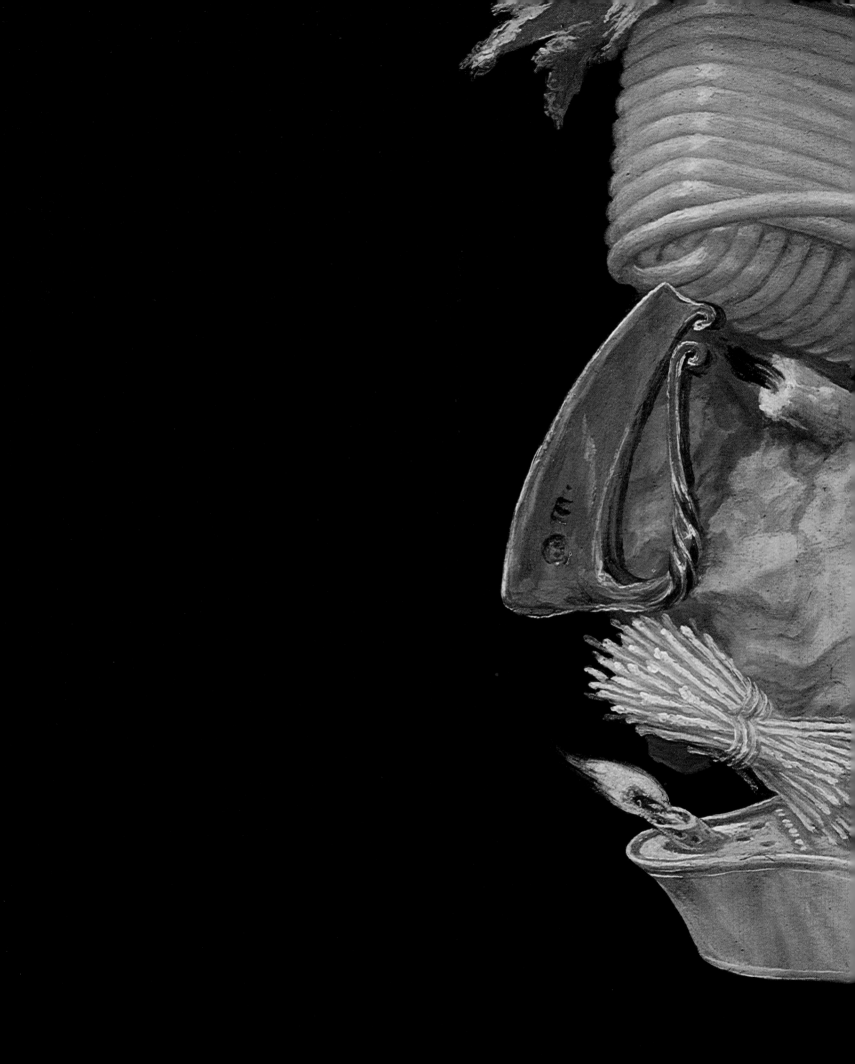

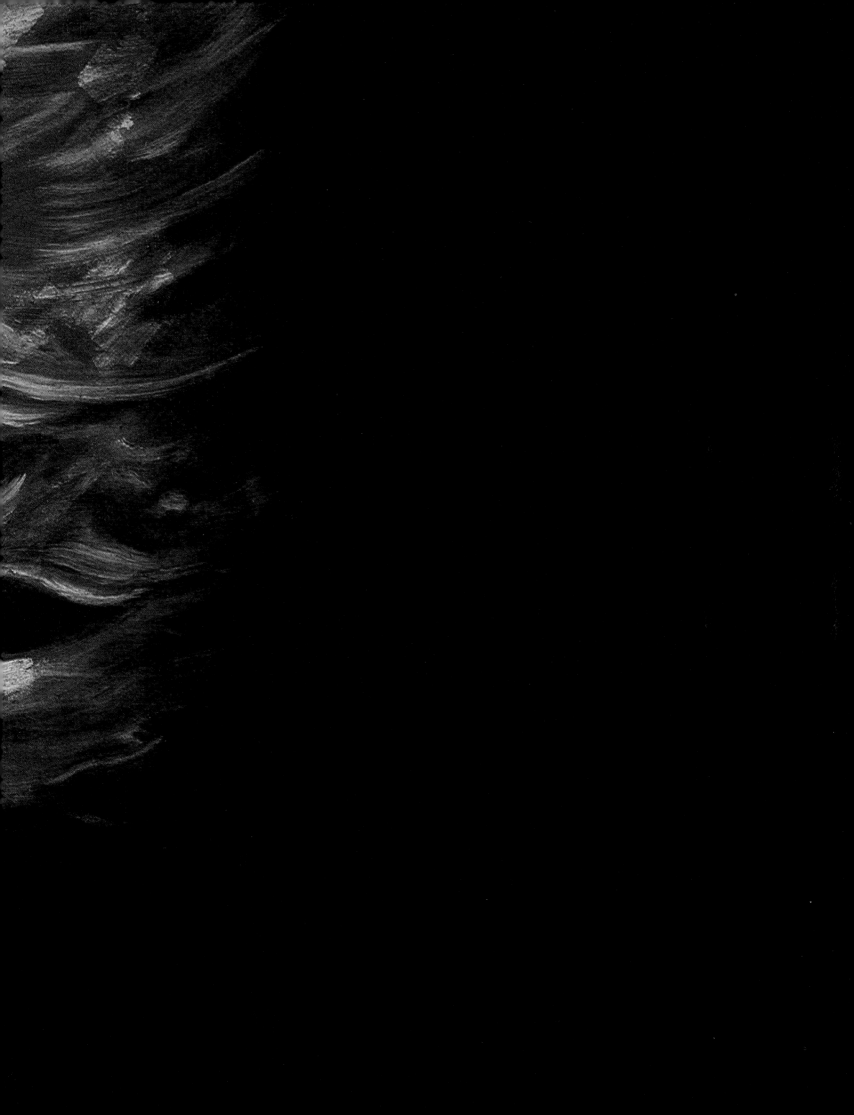

We must mention the much-discussed pen drawing that became known at the sale in 1913 of the collection of Vincent van Gogh. It was first attributed—erroneously, to be sure—to Arcimboldo, then to Heinrich Göding. The drawing, now lost, represents *The Four Elements* after Arcimboldo's paintings, and it seems to have been made hastily by someone who, having seen the original pictures, wanted to save them or memorize them. This would explain the similarities and the differences, both too obvious for us to miss.

Arcimboldo's oeuvre, long restricted to *The Four Seasons* and *The Four Elements*, has now broken loose from the limits formerly imposed on it. The real surprise came this time from paintings in Swedish collections; these reveal the artist's true stature, and have been made known to us thanks to Olof Granberg's *General Inventory of Art Treasures in Sweden*, published in Stockholm in 1911. The interest that this inventory deserves, not to mention the oeuvre and even the name of Arcimboldo, has developed only slowly.

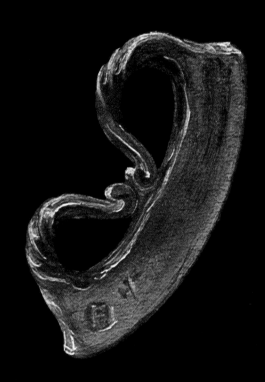

The Golden Fleece (detail of *Fire*)

All of these paintings now in Sweden have their common origin in one event, the sack of Prague in 1648, when the Bohemian capital was partly burned and the Hradcany Castle pillaged after the victory of the Swedish troops, on the orders of Marshal Carl Gustav Wrangel and the count of Koenigsmark. Many of Arcimboldo's works reappeared in Skokloster Castle in Sweden, the residence of Marshal Wrangel, who had his pick of the booty transported there.

Chronologically, the earliest Arcimboldo painting seems to be the admirable *Librarian* (page 13); it is not too far-fetched to call it also his first composite head. Painted in 1562 at the latest (whereas the first series of *The Four Seasons*, in Vienna, is dated 1563), it might have been preceded slightly by the *Self-Portrait* (page 9): the curtain in that work reminds us of the blue damask fabric draped behind the head and over the shoulder of the pile of books that is *The Librarian*. So splendid is the result of this experiment (and surely so great was its success) that it naturally formed the core of the artist's style and subject matter for the rest of his

The Cook

career. Playful it is, this extraordinary canvas which "raises the curtain" on a series or family of allegorical figures that perennially intrigue us. But if the joke here is plain, plainer than in the others, let us agree that it is an excellent one! The open book whose waving pages are the disheveled hair; the beautiful parchment bindings stamped with gold ornament; the marten-tails (used for dusting books) suavely simulating the beard and mustache; the six bookmarks that become five flattened fingers of the trick hand; the eyes made of lenses, good for discerning the indecipherable—all these discoveries of the master painter, his name proudly evoked in the great A of the bold pyramidal shape, make a joyous panegyric to artifice. Is this same joy, this delight that is so wild and intelligent, to be found in his later works? I am not sure that it is. Let us add for the record that in Sweden there are two other *Librarians*, not mentioned by Granberg; it is not easy to decide if they are old and good copies or original replicas—pillaged in either case. One puzzling fact is that they contain small errors or slight variations of detail that could have been made

intentionally, just as small shifts provide marks of originality that later distinguish replicas of *The Four Seasons* which are otherwise identical.

The Jurist, dated 1566 and belonging to a Swedish collection (pages 43, 45), puts us even more frankly in the realm of jest. In 1903 the painting was published in a Swiss religious newspaper by a minister, A. Mohr; a Lausanne resident named E. Doumergue identified it at once as a portrait of John Calvin. This identification was recently refuted in Sven Alfons' fine essay, the best work on Arcimboldo that I know, and it does not stand up under attack; a Swiss theologian from Vaud, after all, will see Calvin's face in every wall smudge and oil slick. There is no real resemblance at all to Calvin, neither in the face nor in the clothing, which is a beautiful fur-lined mantle, not a severe black cloak. And it is unlikely that Emperor Maximilian would have commissioned a caricature of the French religious reformer, for he was very careful to deal tactfully with his dangerous neighbors, the Protestant princes. Moreover Comanini clearly describes the painting in *Il*

Figino, telling of the court's amusement in looking at the portrait of "…a Doctor whose face was so ruined by the French disease that all he had left was a little skin on his chin.… Arcimboldo made him entirely of roasted meats and fish, and the result was such that whoever looked at it saw at once that it was the true portrait of the good old Jurist." The word "doctor," through another confusion, has led some to think that a physician is represented, but Comanini also refers to "legista," which can only mean a doctor of laws. This would account for the flat bag containing the folded papers that are spread under the figure's chin (trial minutes, or notarized or legal documents). Perhaps the black cap covering the head is to hide scars left by the pox, like those so delicately represented on the face by the usual roughened skin of plucked chickens. The eye of *The Jurist* (page 47), another of Arcimboldo's famous eyes, coincides with the eye of the poor little chicken, still pitifully alive. The canvas, which probably had to be restored from poor condition, is signed both on front and back. (Let us note, incidentally, that the signature on the

91

Plate (pages 49, 53), is so close in manner to *The Jurist* that it must belong to the same time. Cooked meats make up this composite head, a suckling pig and assorted poultry. In either sense the head between the plate and its lid is crowned by a kind of military helmet: an oak branch sprouts like a soldierly plume into the air when it is above; when below, this becomes only a table ornament near the lemon slice and toothpicks on the rim of the plate. Turned one way, the man's eye and that of the little chicken are superimposed; turned the other way, the bird's illuminated tailpiece becomes the pupil of an eye peering from beneath arched brows paved with teeth—in the first position, these form the old soldier's jaw. I am disconcerted by the fingers of the

The Man and the Vegetables

lovely hands reflected in the metal as they hold the lid—their softness is both cruel and tender, too emphasized not to be one more allusion to the duplicity of the whole. Although the procedure of alternating two pictures by inverting the panel is a not uncommon sport, *The Man in the Plate* stands out as an oddity in Arcimboldo's work. Without pushing the matter too far toward symbolism, which would be easy to do, I would say that in this vigorous representation it is the fiercely poetical aspect of the act of discovery that continually charms me as I contemplate the reproduction.

The small invertible painting in the Museo Civico of Cremona is often called *The Gardener*, but I prefer the title *The Man and the Vegetables* (pages 93, 95). It is actually quite different from *The Man in the Plate*, although the artist exploits the same technique. It comes to us not by way of the Swedish sack of Prague, but through an early acquisition by the museum under circumstances never clarified. For a number of reasons the date of the work could only be in the last period of the artist's career, after his return to his native country

The Man and the Vegetables (inverted)

in 1587. Held one way, it is a charming still life of vegetables arranged in a bowl: radishes, turnips, onions, dandelions, russula mushrooms, chestnuts in their husks, walnuts, and hazelnuts. Ah, but invert the canvas and you have a chubby, mirthful head with a walnut and hazelnut for eyes and two russula mushrooms for scarlet lips. In the choice of components and their rendering, this painting rather resembles the splendid *Vertumnus* (which I will soon discuss), so one must grant their comparable origin in place and time. Perhaps the painter, with his usual generosity, gave it to some friend who brought it to Cremona.

Two canvases by Arcimboldo, *The Cook* and *The Cellarman* (pages 87, 89), which were in Prague before World War II, are heads composed of the tools of their trade. These allegories strike me as more Germanic and comical in flavor than the works that thrill us with their originality; the authenticity of both, however, is not in question. They would have fared better if they had not been overlooked by the Swedes in 1648, for both have disappeared since the catastrophic episode in

96

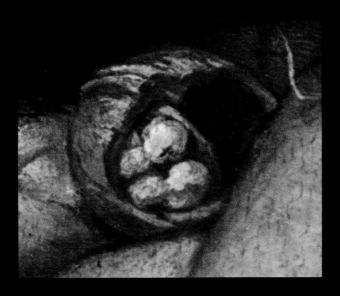

The Man and the Vegetables (detail of eye)

modern Czech history. Now we must regrettably make them out from old black-and-white photographs, somewhat obscure in detail.

But the greatest treasure in the seventeenth-century Swedish collections, or spoils, is the *Vertumnus* (pages 101–7, 109). With the help of descriptions by Lomazzo and Comanini, both friends of the artist, this work has been recognized as the *Portrait of Rudolf II*. The portrait was admittedly conceived in jest as much as in homage, but to whom goes the greater honor, to the model or the artist? The court painter knew for sure that the all-powerful emperor would have nothing but satisfaction at seeing himself portrayed entirely in fruits and vegetables. Let us recall the stupidity of Louis XIV, indignant at the sight of Bernini's prodigious equestrian statue of him. Indeed! And if Arcimboldo's picture moves us, and does more to glorify Rudolf than any known portrait ever did for the Sun King, it is because love speaks here rather than respect, because the artist's keen admiration takes the form of a joyous embrace rather than a reverent bow or prostration.

The solar star that ripens the beautiful fruits and vegetables in the garden of perfect sympathy, this is Rudolf as we see him here. His eyes—a mulberry for his right one, a black cherry for his left—watch us from beneath beanpod and peapod eyebrows; and the melon forehead, peach and apple cheeks, pear nose, hazelnut mustache, and bristly chestnut-burr chin all invest this figure with a kind of majestic brilliance unequaled in any other royal portrait. The crown, fashioned of fruits and berries of every description (golden spikes of grain, grapes, currants, pomegranates, wormwood, olives, cherries, figs, and medlars), emanates mystery as no jeweled crown of gold could do. And all of this thanks to Arcimboldo's passionate contemplation—contemplation through his mind's eye, I make haste to add, since he executed the painting in Milan after his final departure from Bohemia had taken him far from the emperor's physical presence.

The commentaries and descriptions by Comanini and Lomazzo, in prose and verse, show us Arcimboldo in the process of completing the *Vertumnus* about 1590. He had just sent Emperor Rudolf another painting which the two writers also discuss at length: I shall call it the first *Flora*. The *Portrait of Rudolf II as Vertumnus* joined *Flora* in Prague a little later, only to be carried off in 1648 by the troops of Wrangel and Koenigsmark. It is probable that Comanini's lengthy poem dedicated to "Vertumnus" (published in 1591 in *Il Figino*) went to Prague with the painting that had inspired it. Rudolf's delight when he opened this package, as I imagine it, is proved by the simple fact that this was when he made the sixty-four-year-old Arcimboldo a count palatine.

We are left now with a last work, *The Nymph Flora*—or rather the *Floras,* for it seems certain to me that these graceful goddesses are at least two (pages 113–15). Comanini's *Il Figino* and Lomazzo's writings—clumsy by comparison—again give us our first news of such a *Flora,* a woman in full face or three-quarters, her head and neck composed mostly of white flowers

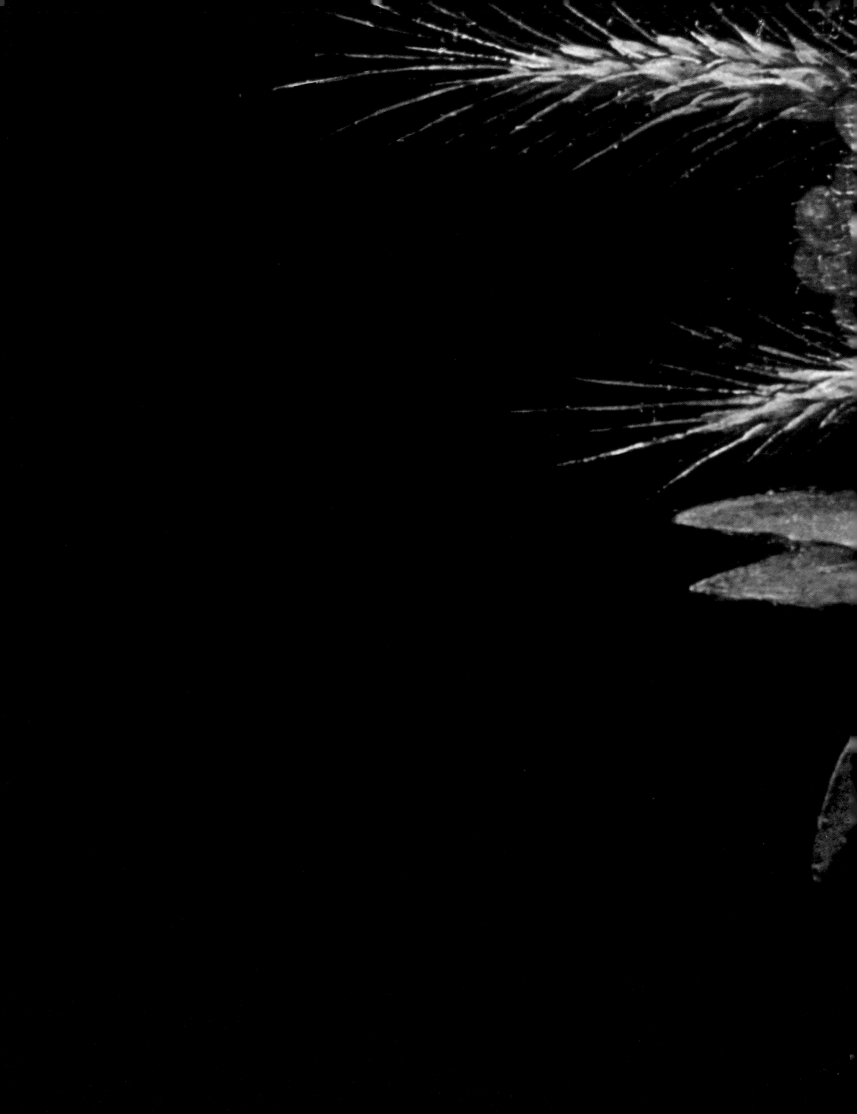

and her clothing of green leaves. Painted by Arcimboldo in Milan, Lomazzo tells us, in response to a wish of Rudolf II rather than in fulfillment of a commission, the work must be contemporary with *The Man and the Vegetables* in Cremona. I would date it approximately 1587 or 1588, and thus the first work of Arcimboldo's final "Italian" period. It was sent to Prague without delay, where it later became part of the Swedish booty when the capital was sacked. Certainly this was the panel in the photograph published by Sven Alfons when it was discovered in a Stockholm collection (it is now in London). On the back of the painting one reads an old inscription: *La Flora dell' Arcimboldo*.

The admiration that his friends and contemporaries had for the painting is amply documented by three madrigals: one by Comanini in *Il Figino*, the second by Gherardini (Arcimboldo's guest in Milan), and a third by Gherardo Borgogni. Of these we present the first (sometimes reprinted inaccurately), followed by its translation:

Portrait of Rudolf II as Vertumnus

Son io Flora, o pur fiori?
Se fior, come di Flora
Ho col sembiante il riso? E s'io son Flora,
Come Flora è sol fiori?
Ah! non fiori son io, non io son Flora.
Anzi son Flora, e fiori.
Fior mille, una sol Flora;
Vivi fior, viva Flora.
Però, che i fior fan Flora, e Flora i fiori,
Sai come? I fiori in Flora
Cangiò saggio Pittore, e Flora in fiori.

Am I Flora, or am I flowers?
If I be flowers, how then can Flora
Have a smiling face? And if I be Flora,
How can Flora be only flowers?
Ah! I am not flowers, nor am I Flora,
Yet Flora I am, and flowers.
A thousand flowers, a single Flora,
Living flowers, a living Flora.
But if flowers make Flora, and Flora flowers,
Do you know how? The flowers into Flora
The wise painter changed, and Flora into
    flowers.

In the second madrigal, Gherardini (in Lomazzo's *Idea*, Milan, 1590) laments the disappearance of the beautiful *Flora*—that is, to Prague—and seems to allude to a replacement or substitute. Now there is a picture in the Robert Lebel collection in Paris that precisely corresponds to the old descriptions of *The Nymph Flora*, although there is no inscription on the back of the panel (made of Italian wood); certain minor differences on the front, such as the addition of a yellow lily on the breast, show that this might very likely be a later copy, and probably superior in quality. What matters in a work by Arcimboldo—the sensitive tones, harmonized with such exquisite sweetness that the soft and delicate skin evokes the Italian word *morbidezza;* the unusual look of the dark eyes set in rosebud sockets and brightened with tiny white petals; the special joy in the full-blooming lilies (white and orange in the headdress, yellow on the corsage) as well as the graceful budding lily that forms the nose above the rosebud lips; the harmonious drawing of the nape, tiny pale-pink flowers nestled in an open bed of

111

round white petals; and the perfection of the floral mosaic of which the face and neck are built—everything seems to me to speak for, to proclaim, the authenticity of the painting. Compared with the allegorical girl in *Spring* (see pages 17, 19), the Lebel *Flora* shows a figure that is constructed of nearly the same elements but in this case more finished, more advanced toward what I call the floral mosaic of the flesh; the leafy texture of *Flora*'s lovely garment of greenery, too, now seems thicker.

The third and somewhat confused madrigal by Borgogni (Bergamo, 1592)—written in Lombard dialect rather than Tuscan, which does not help the understanding of it—leads us to believe that the *Flora* in his poem may have been Arcimboldo's last work, painted after the *Vertumnus* had been sent away; at this time the artist probably felt the need to have one of his beautiful paintings before his eyes, within his reach. For the melancholy of an artist who has become separated from everything that his hands have made at the dictates of his mind is un-

Flora

bearably sad. I sense the response to such a melancholy in the expression of the *Flora* in Paris, which, if it indeed is the second one, could be dated 1591.

Does it help to add that there exists another *Flora,* with bare breast? I will not call it *Flora III*, because the reproductions of it are unconvincing and suggest nothing but an "arcimboldesque." "Arcimboldism" and "arcimboldesque" paintings, too often praised in order to flatter collectors and art dealers, have not and will not be discussed in this book; I have already stated my reasons above. All that I wish here is to have lifted the veil a little on the person and art of Giuseppe Arcimboldo, a subject so marvelous (again the right word) that it should be isolated from its context so as to be seen more clearly, instead of being smothered by kith and kin.

But you will ask: How are we to understand, or simply grasp, this art, this output of seventeen known original paintings (and about thirty, if we include the authentic replicas), once so famous, then all but forgotten, and now back in favor during the

last half-century because their "fantastic" character puts them among the "forerunners of Surrealism"? I for one am not afflicted with the passion to classify, and I believe that if one loves and respects the history of art it must be allowed a little chaos. In this vast arena the art of Arcimboldo, to my eyes, stands out like a fixed and dazzling point— enticing, exalting, and even reassuring, for in its uniqueness his work is perfected like that of only the greatest artists.

"Mannerism": I do not quarrel with this label, since usage applies the term to very nearly his entire century, but Arcimboldo's paintings never attempt to tell a story or recount a dream, as do almost all others in this style. Nor do I object to "Baroque," for he has the power to shock and a taste for masquerading, yet I see nothing convulsive in his work. "Pre-Romantic" I would likewise grant, because he uses natural elements, but it is only a usage and shows little feeling for nature as a whole, nor ever inclines toward the lyrical. I like "Fantastic" provided the formula is used only in contrast to Plato's "icastic," or figurative realism

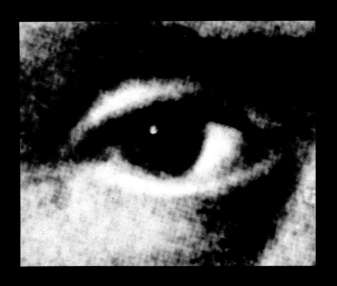

Self-Portrait (detail of eye)

(in the *Sophist*), as Father Comanini used it for
Arcimboldo in his neo-Platonic dialogue, *Il Figino*.
"Pre-Surrealist," like Hieronymus Bosch (that
most surreal of old masters), as Arcimboldo has so
often been proclaimed? I herewith deny this, for
nothing in Arcimboldo smacks of the unconscious,
whether automatic or oneiric, as I see it, nor does
anything in the structured accumulations of his
composite heads point to the jarring, antagonistic
associations so typical of Surrealism (as, for
example, in Lautréamont's famous *Chants de
Maldoror*). "Playful," even humorous? I admit
these willingly, provided we do not adopt the
shortsighted view of his contemporaries—including such friends as Comanini, Morigia, and
Lomazzo—who abused the category of "joker"
as an apology for nonconformism in an age of
insecurity. Finally "Symbolist," the most recent
interpretation: before modern criticism, our
contemporaries mostly had recourse to this, to the
point of finding that the animals comprising *Earth*,
for example, were allusions to the complicated
tendencies in human character. I do not oppose this,

but I allot no great importance to a viewpoint so dependent on the allegorical images that were spread by the taste for iconologies, and I refuse to accept Arcimboldo's work as a collection of symbols. These alleged "keys" can only falsify or diminish the brilliance of the work they have been applied to, work in no way obscure.

Far more important seems the form taken by the anthropomorphic still life and shared by nearly all of Arcimboldo's composite heads and other paintings (including the two invertible canvases); endowed with their own life by the subtle artifice of their composition, these still lifes are another "marvel" among the products of only this artist's palette and brushes. What a pity that Charles Sterling, so great an expert on seventeenth-century still lifes in Spain and Flanders, did not see the splendor of Arcimboldo's, and acknowledged *The Man and the Vegetables* as only a joke "worthy of being placed next to a grotesque fetus in a cabinet of curiosities." Without commenting further, as one could, on the questionable use of the adjective "grotesque," I point here to the indignation of this responsible critic when faced with a phenomenon that he considers inadmissible—the still life brought to life, "humanized." For on the contrary this pictorial phenomenon enthralls me, as today it apparently enthralls more and more persons for whom art has become inspiration, a source of joy.

But there is more: when we observe what I have already called this phenomenon, which in the best sense of the word it is, we are eventually led to notice in Arcimboldo's paintings the use of a third, if not even a fourth dimension. By third dimension I mean the distance that must intervene between the observer and the painting before he ceases to see still-life elements (fruit, flowers, land and sea creatures, tools, and various materials) and perceives the entirety of a human face, whether graceful, stately, haughty, or ludicrous. In the fourth dimension I take account of the minutes or seconds the observer needs to bridge the gap that separates him from the point or moment when this transformation takes place in his vision. Thus the concept of volume, or at least spatial relief, and some sense of time have been introduced onto the painted surface, which is truly uncommon even for that exotic capital of Bohemia in the sixteenth century.

To the question of whether Arcimboldo was aware of all the new factors in his art, I would answer that I think so: although this man is to a degree inexplicable, he also seems to me one of the least limited who ever lived and painted. If we were to compare him with someone of our time, I rather think my choice would be Braque. In the one and in the other I see truly great artists, both sure enough in the originality of their invention and the flawlessness of their craft to carry out their work without haste or shortcuts. Simply and profoundly, with a kind of solemn love and proud finality they follow the unique impulsion of their own imagination.

As I bid farewell, with regret, to the marvelous Arcimboldo, I place next to his name that of my friend Yasha David, his ardent admirer. To him I owe the idea for this book, its title, its arrangement, and the documentation that I have used in writing it. To him we should give thanks.

A. P. de M.

CATALOGUE OF PAINTINGS

Summer. 1572 version. Oil on canvas, 35½ x 28⅜"
(90 x 72 cm). Signed and dated front, GIVSEPPE
ARCIMBOLDO•F•1572. Whereabouts unknown
Summer. 1573 version. Oil on canvas, 29 x 24" (73.6 x
61 cm). Signed and dated front, GIVSEPPE
ARCIMBOLDO•F•1573. Private collection, London

27 *Autumn.* 1573 version, with garland. Oil on canvas
(remounted), 30⅛ x 25¼" (76.5 x 64 cm). Musée du
Louvre, Paris
Autumn. 1572 version. Oil on canvas, 35½ x 27½"
(90 x 70 cm). Private collection, Paris
Autumn. 1573 version. Oil on canvas, 29 x 24"
(73.6 x 61 cm). Private collection, London

33 *Winter.* 1573 version, with garland. Oil on canvas
(remounted), 30⅛ x 25¼" (76.5 x 64 cm). Musée du
Louvre, Paris
Winter. 1563 version. Oil on wood, 26¼ x 19⅞" (66.6 x
50.5 cm). Signed front, GIVSEPPE
ARCIMBOLDO•F; on reverse, 1563•HJEMS.
Kunsthistorisches Museum, Vienna
Winter. 1572 version. Oil on canvas, 35½ x 27½"
(90 x 70 cm). Private collection, New York
Winter. 1573 version. Oil on canvas, 29 x 24"
(73.6 x 61 cm). Private collection, London

43 *The Jurist.* 1566. Oil on canvas (remounted), 25¼ x
20⅛" (64 x 51 cm). Signed front (on book), G•
ARCIMBOLDO; on reverse, 1566 GIU
•ARCIMBOLDO. Gripsholm Slott, Sweden

49 *The Man in the Plate (The Cook).* c. 1567. Oil on wood
(invertible), 20⅝ x 16⅛" (52.5 x 41 cm). Private
collection, Stockholm

57 *Air.* c. 1571. Oil on canvas, 29½ x 22¼" (75 x 56.5 cm). Private collection, London

61 *Earth.* c. 1570. Oil on wood, 27⅝ x 19¼" (70.2 x 48.7 cm). Private collection, Vienna

71 *Water.* c. 1568. Oil on wood, 26⅛ x 19⅞" (66.5 x 50.5 cm). On reverse, AQUA. Kunsthistorisches Museum, Vienna
    Water (without pearl necklace). Oil on canvas, 25¼ x 20⅞" (64 x 53 cm). Private collection, Brussels

77 *Fire.* 1566. Oil on wood, 26⅛ x 20⅛" (66.5 x 51 cm). Signed front (on cannon), JOSEPHUS ARCIMBOLDUS MLNENSIS•F.; on reverse, IGNIS 1566. Kunsthistorisches Museum, Vienna

87 *The Cook.* c. 1574. Oil on canvas, 26⅜ x 20½" (67 x 52 cm). Formerly Collection Müller, Prague

89 *The Cellarman.* c. 1574. Oil on canvas, 26⅜ x 20½" (67 x 52 cm). Formerly Collection Müller, Prague

93 *The Man and the Vegetables (The Gardener).* c. 1590. Oil on wood (invertible), 13¾ x 9½" (35 x 24 cm). Museo Civico, Cremona

109 *Portrait of Rudolf II as Vertumnus.* c. 1590. Oil on wood, 27¾ x 22⅞" (70.5 x 58 cm). Skokloster Slott, Sweden

    Flora (without yellow lily on chest). c. 1588. Oil on wood, 30 x 22⅝" (76.3 x 57.5 cm). On reverse, LA FLORA DELL'ARCIMBOLDO. Private collection, London

113 *Flora.* c. 1591. Oil on wood, 28¾ x 22¼" (73 x 56.5 cm). Collection Robert Lebel, Paris

128